Media Relations and Creative Marketing Tips for Financial Professionals

I0485244

Media Relations and Creative Marketing Tips for Financial Professionals

Joseph Finora

2007

For further information, additional copies or a
no-obligation consultation, contact Joseph Finora at: jfinora@optonline.net
All calls, consultations and client list are kept confidential.

www.josephfinora.com

Media Relations and Creative Marketing Tips
for Financial Professionals

To the most important people in my life:

Mary Grace, Joey, James and Gabrielle

Contents

Introduction
Why I Wrote This Little Book
or
Putting Big Ideas in a Small Package

I wrote this little book because nobody else did, despite the fact that there's a giant need for the information it contains.

The truth is there are plenty of books in circulation about marketing and media relations and lots of courses available that anyone could take. The problem is that most of these books and courses either don't cater to the special needs of financial professionals or are simply too big and complicated to meet the basic marketing and media-relations needs—which I aim to do here.

Most financial professionals don't have the time or inclination to immerse themselves in a full-range media and marketing strategy. Here I've given them what they need to know, based on my 20+ years in this business as a marketing and communications professional, in a direct and concise manner. With the information on the following pages, you'll be able to launch a basic marketing and media-relations strategy yourself or intelligently talk about one with an outside professional you may consider hiring.

Drawing on Experience

As the saying goes, I've worked both sides of the street. I started in this business as a financial journalist during the bull market of the late 1980's and into the mid-1990's. To say this gave me a great education is an understatement. As a journalist, I was able to see numerous Wall St. firms operate, both large and small, and meet some brilliant and not-so brilliant people in a way few of us are ever able to do so.

I then moved "inside" taking a position as a writer and later a media-relations representative at a blue-chip firm. I gradually moved on to other firms and in my most recent position, was in charge of corporate communications for a triple-A rated, worldwide, financial-services and insurance firm. My particular specialty—and one of the most enjoyable aspects of the job—was helping to get the company's broker-dealer and its numerous independent representatives favorably portrayed in the trade and consumer media. It was a challenging and enjoyable assignment.

Having worked for many years as a Wall St. "beat reporter," has given me an immeasurable advantage. I know most of the reporters and editors who cover Wall St. and they know me. I know what they want— qualified leads, informed sources—and refuse to waste their time. The result has been a very lively and fruitful media-relations strategy that's added a great deal of value and integrity to a firm that sorely lacked it but desperately deserved it. In this little book I hope to be able to share some of these same ideas with you so your own practice can flourish.

Welcome to the Worlds of Marketing and Media Relations

Very little can compare to the thrill of seeing one's name positively portrayed in the newspaper. While it often gives a slight rush of excitement to see yourself quoted as an "expert" or "authority," imagine what it can do for your business.

We all enjoy being perceived as experts in our fields—it's a nice compliment to the ego and the recognition shows that our hard work has paid off. In addition to the small amount of celebrity status it brings, being called on by a reporter or television show producer lends credibility and exposure—both are valuable items which can be leveraged into business growth—the main reason to pursue a comprehensive media-relations strategy.

Happy about seeing your name in the paper? Don't just show it to your mother. Think of how you'll feel when you hand a client or prospect a copy of a trade magazine article where you are quoted as an expert source. How do you think that client or prospect will feel about seeing your name in print? This is far more impressive than showing someone a copy of an advertisement you paid for or a direct mail piece you distributed. Not that those aren't legitimate means of promotion— they are—yet media relations adds far greater prestige since the writer thought to call and ask for your professional opinion. The writer has his or her name on the piece, taking responsibility for the article and by doing so is indirectly endorsing you. It's safe to say that your image in that customer's or prospect's eyes has probably considerably grown and he or she will most likely feel comfortable not only doing business with you but will probably offer some referrals—if it's part of your practice to accept them.

Seeing one's name negatively portrayed in the paper is an unbelievably devastating feeling. This usually occurs because a poor risk was taken or bad judgment exercised. We address this concern later in our chapter on "risk" and "spin."

Enough about the rewards. What's it take to obtain them?

Like investing, a successful marketing and/or media-relations strategy requires a long-term commitment and in return, can pay long-term dividends. However, to enjoy those dividends you must be prepared to invest daily in the process—or pay a professional to do so—and have the following:

- A clear message
- A basic media kit
- An understanding of media needs
- A willingness to follow-up and make yourself available to reporters.

Initially, it's very unlikely that reporters will call you. It's more likely that you will have to take the initiative and contact them via telephone, mail or both. But before you pick up the phone and call The Wall Street Journal editorial desk, ask yourself:

- In what area am I an expert? (i.e.: On which subjects can I authoritatively talk?)
- What is it about myself or my practice that's different or distinctive from that of my competitors?
- In what unique or outstanding ways have my business skills helped my clients? My community?

The answers to these questions are intertwined. Chances are you're an expert in at least one area—life insurance, tax planning, retirement planning, trusts and estates, college funding etc. Were you bearish when everyone else was bullish? Were you advising clients about Real Estate Investment Trusts long before they became fashionable? Did you caution clients against following the "hot" investments of the day and keep them in sensible securities? These are all ideas that can become stories about you.

Moving on Your Strengths

When business is up, marketing and media relations tend to take on a less important role than they do when times are tough. It's a mistake to lighten up on your strategy just because business is brisk. Everything changes.

Similarly, jumping into a marketing and media-relations plan in the middle of a down market will get you into the game late. When the economy slows customers become apprehensive and take longer to close deals. The smart marketers keep the program running all the time so when a recession hits, they're ready. Nothing forces people to re-examine their holdings faster than a few quarters of negative returns, which is why all the pieces of your media-relations and marketing strategy need to be operating all the time.

You're generally better off maintaining a steady course in your media-relations and marketing efforts. Always keep your goals in mind and you'll operate a more efficient business because you can always build market share—in up and down markets. Don't wait for the "inevitable rebound," there's no telling when (or if) it will come. There's a general practice of cutting back on marketing when the economic climate gets tough. That's usually a mistake. Think about the big marketers like Coca Cola, McDonald's, IBM and the automobile manufacturers. They keep telling the world their message no matter what the economic climate. You can too. And you should.

Reach out to your local newspapers and radio stations. Address local groups. Talk to everyone you meet about what you do. Hand out business cards and newspaper clips highlighting your areas of expertise. Drop off flyers wherever you can. Talk to related professionals such as accountants, attorneys, insurance agents etc. Consider everyone and every situation an opportunity to market your practice. I once picked up a marketing account for a winery after striking up a conversation with the tour guide. It led to several profitable assignments. With a little imagination, determination and communication, you can do the same.

In a down market, think about cross-selling and up-selling opportunities, new products and services you can add and most importantly, think about what your clients may need. Then, get in touch with them. The following pages will show you how.

Use Available Resources

Your broker-dealer or other firms with whom you choose to do business may be able to help you in basic marketing and media relations. Often they have a staff (it may be one person in some shops) that produces a variety of marketing material and can possibly help you reach the desired media outlets. Very often reporters call the broker-dealer's media relations contact—sometimes listed as Corporate Communications Representative. Find out who that person is and let him or her know what your goals are. At the very least, he or she should take your contact information and pass it on to a reporter when the right opportunity presents itself. Or they can direct you to an outside firm or freelancer who specializes in your area.

Most of the major product manufacturers—mutual fund and insurance companies—create a large amount of marketing material that's available for the asking. The caveat: it'll be difficult not mentioning their product(s) in whatever you do.

Say you're interested in holding a seminar on investing for women. Many firms have special programs geared exclusively for this and other specialty areas. They'll usually provide things like postcards, advertising slicks, prospecting and follow-up letters, posters, talking points, a telephone script, and often a Powerpoint and video presentation—all compliance-approved. They may even supply a guest speaker if your group is large enough. Obviously, there is a great advantage to having material already prepared and one you may want to consider.

Or, your broker-dealer may supply similar compliance-approved material that does not promote any particular firm's products or services. The choice is yours and it depends on how you want to be portrayed. Study what's available. Experiment. Think carefully about how you would feel should you receive such material as a prospect one day or listen to such a talk. Would you feel the material presented was unbiased and presented in your best interest? Or does it look and feel like its too heavily pushing product? These are the things that will form your clients' and prospects' first (and often lasting) impressions of you and effect how you are perceived in your local business community. The simple (and usually best) answer: put the clients first and you'll almost always both be happy.

Nearly all marketing and media-relations programs boil down to one simple question: How do you wish to be perceived? Do you want to be seen as a "product pusher" or a thoughtful, sincere and honest businessperson who regularly strives to find the best for his/her clients? The answer, I hope, is obvious.

Note: A marketing or media kit is generally packaged in a pocket folder. A custom folder can usually be printed by a local shop at minimal cost. I recommend this as it helps distinguish your press kit from the pile that usually accumulates on nearly every reporter's desk.

Should you decide to produce your media kit yourself, be sure to have it professionally proofread before you print it. Your printer should be able to help you find a proofreader or you can call a local newspaper or check the telephone directory.

Chapter 1

Getting Started
Putting Press Releases to Work

Have you increased your advertising budget, invested in a new sign, begun offering new products or services, added new software or increased staff? These are good ideas but unless you're one of a select group of innovative marketers, you're ignoring one of the oldest, most effective and least expensive forms of self-promotion ever created — the press release.

What's a Press Release?

A press release is a brief description of a person, product or service your business is offering that is sent to appropriate media outlets as a possible news item. It is not advertising. Don't treat it as such. The curiosity and interest a press release may generate is primarily aimed at increasing awareness and indirectly at growing sales.

Are press releases effective? Look at it this way. Just about every corporation in America uses them to circulate news about itself.

The amount invested is a fraction of what is spent for advertising but when done properly, the costs can be far outweighed by the benefits. Press releases have been designed to be great marketing tools, as well as legitimate news items to get your name in the local newspaper, or on radio or cable television programs. If the big guys think they can profit from them, so can you.

It's never been written that one must be a giant corporation in order to issue a press release. Many smaller concerns have enjoyed success with press releases for years when trying to promote their product, office or services. Unfortunately, press releases have been grossly under-utilized as a marketing tool by many financial professionals. But as the business grows more competitive and media relations become an increasingly important part of a firm's growth strategy, the value of press releases will also increase. A press release can be just the item to help your business stand out from the crowd.

The Press Release Advantage

What's the advantage of a press release? Why not just take out an ad? Advertising space or radio/television time is purchased with the sole intention of increasing sales. Everyone knows this and is naturally slightly suspicious of advertising—no matter how honest you may be. However, when an editor or news producer thinks enough of a person, product or service to actually treat it as news, that's a real compliment and in the mind of the public—delivers trust—something that not even the best advertising can conclusively buy.

The reason for this is simple: when people see or hear a legitimate news person covering an item as opposed to a paid advertisement/ endorsement, it has near-instant credibility—something that doesn't usually come with advertising.

Can't I just Use the Phone?

Too busy to write? Sure, you can try phoning reporters and editors to promote your business but this method is generally practiced by those with an established press relationship. A professional media relations person should have enough contacts to be able to do so on your behalf.

That doesn't mean phoning will not work for you—it may. Reporters are generally appreciative of those who call with legitimate news items, however, it can be difficult getting them on the phone. With a press release they have the luxury of reading it when they're ready to do so and give thought to the item and then decide if they'd like further information. While the phone does work both ways, telephoning reporters is generally for those with established media relationships. It's also been my experience that unsolicited e-mails too easily fall victim to the delete key. This doesn't mean they can't work either but judging from my experience, the basic press release, sent first-class mail, is often the best method for getting your media-relations plan started.

Be aware that telephone calls can also takes up a large amount of your time. However, should a reporter or editor call you, remember they are often on deadline. Be sure to answer them in a prompt and courteous manner.

Chapter 2

Getting Noticed

W hat's the first step in preparing a press release? Look around. What's newsworthy about your business? About yourself? It can be as simple as a new product or service your business is now offering or it can be as complicated as estate planning for wealthy individuals.

Other often newsworthy items include charitable activities. Are you providing free financial-planning help to people with low incomes? Are you teaching high school students finance basics? Will you be hosting a fundamental tax-strategy seminar? These are the types of things that have made news and often increased visibility of a business in the process. Indirectly, they've often helped fuel sales growth. Use your imagination.

If none of these things apply, start getting creative. Would you be willing to teach a basic course on how Wall St. works to a group of high school students? Would you be willing to counsel local senior citizens on estate-planning basics? How about firefighters or police officers on life insurance or saving for college?

Offer Yourself as an Expert (But Be Sure You Are One)

If you answered "yes" to any of the questions or if they've helped you consider what you can offer, start thinking about the appropriate outlets. Call the police station or PTA. Tell them your idea and gauge their reaction. You'd be surprised how cooperative people can be. Then once your plan is in place, contact the appropriate media representatives.

One good idea is to offer your expertise to local media outlets. Local newspapers and radio stations are often the easiest places to start. This will give you exposure as an authority on your area of expertise and at the same time, put your name in front of prospects.

Consider this: Say you've recently installed a new, state-of-the-art money-management platform in your office. That's news. Make a list of the platform's capabilities. The company that produced the platform should have this information and may even have a media-relations office that can help you. Remind them that good publicity for you is also good for them.

Maybe the platform's got a retirement-planning component. Nearly everyone is concerned about how they'll fund their retirement. Then locate which newspapers in your area have lively business or personal-finance sections. I generally advise avoiding "give-away" or free newspapers—the kind you find on your doorstep on Saturday mornings. While they have some readership, you'll usually get far more mileage out of a mention in a paper with a paid circulation rather than the local (and free) shopper. The reason? People read and trust papers they've paid for. Free newspapers are discarded at a much higher frequency than are those that people purchase. Other outlets may be newsletters that reach the groups you're hoping to target. These should be your media "hit list."

Once you've created this list prepare the actual release. Editors are regularly in search of news that will benefit their readers because that's what sells papers. At the same time, they are usually deluged with press releases and announcements that are inappropriate for their readership. They do not appreciate blatant, amateurish attempts to use them as your personal publicity vehicle.

What this means is that your press release has got to look professional and has got to contain real news. There are some basic items that no press release should be without:

A. The Release Date: This lets the editor know it's o.k. to immediately print the enclosed information. Since editors usually work on strict daily or weekly deadlines, most press releases feature the heading, "For Immediate Release." This means it is available upon receipt. This is usually printed on the top right of the release.

B. The Contact: Editors will sometimes call to double check your information if they decide to use it. Their job is made easier if they have someone they can call for verification purposes or for further information. Be sure this person is aware of the release and is well informed on the topic. This can go below the release date or in the upper left corner.

C. Headline: More often than not, this is what makes or breaks the release. If your headline offers real news, there is a good chance it will be read and considered for publication. Don't try to be too clever or cute in this area. As the saying goes: Just the facts. If you're indeed offering a free basic financial plan your headline should be something like this:

XYZ Financial Management Offers Free Basic Financial Plan to Seniors

Don't use an exclamation mark. They are for ads. Do use words like "new, now, how to, exclusive" and "free" when applicable. Use initial caps on your headlines and center them across the page.

D. Body Copy: This is the heart and soul of your announcement. It must be direct and to the point, well written and full of information. Here you must answer the five W's of journalism: "who, what, when, where and why." Make it known if photos, charts, graphs or other illustrative material are available.

After describing the featured item or service be sure to note when it is available, the price(s) and other pertinent data but don't stray from the topic. Editors are generally big adherents of the **KISS** rule: **Keep It So Simple.**

Check and double check your release before it goes out and don't forget the basics like telephone number, website and hours of operation. The release should be double-spaced and well typed. If it's sloppy or lacks basic information, most editors won't take the time to fix it until it's suitable for publication. Without the proper format and follow-up, a press release usually does not make it into print.

Follow-up entails telephone calls and/or additional mailings. It's popular to send releases via fax and e-mail but a professionally laid-out announcement on company stationery makes a better impression and usually stands a greater chance of making it into print.

Try to personalize your release. Attach a personal note to the target editor but keep it short and honest. For example: I am a longtime reader of the Gainesville Gazette. I'm sure you're very busy but was hoping you could take the time to read about our new offer of a Free Basic Financial Plan for Seniors in our community. Feel free to visit our office and see for yourself. We think the seniors in our town are going to be very pleased with this service. Thank you for you time and consideration."

The above note is simple yet personal. It may not sound like much but it's better than "Dear Editor." And with press releases, a little extra effort can pay big dividends.

[Sample Press Release]
XYZ Financial Management Offers Free Basic Financial Plan to Seniors

FOR IMMEDIATE RELEASE Contact: Sam Sample
Tel: 212.222.2222

TOWNSVILLE, —XYZ Financial Management is offering a free, basic financial plan to local seniors. The no-obligation plan, a $500 value, is being offered as a means to help the local senior population better deal with a wide range of personal-finance issues, such as retirement and tax planning, long-term care, trusts, estates and insurance coverage. Model plans will be run on the firm's new financial-planning software, Senior Vision, available only to financial planners. All consultations are confidential.

"With the general age of the population increasing, it's imperative that seniors have access to first-rate financial planning," says Tim Taxman, President of XYZ Financial Management. "Our software will take the realities seniors are facing into account before producing a sensible, long-range plan to help them meet their goals. And one of our advisors will also be on hand to provide the personal touch."

Plans will be made by appointment only from Jan. 15-21. Interested seniors should call ahead to make an appointment and bring all necessary documentation with them, such as tax forms, bank statements and other pertinent financial data. An XYZ Financial representative can also help determine which information seniors should bring to the consultation. After the model plan is produced, an XYZ Financial representative will spend about one hour reviewing the plan and offering suggestions.

XYZ Financial Management has been a member of the Townsville community since 1976 and has helped hundreds of people from all income levels successfully meet today's most pressing financial challenges. Representatives specialize in tax, retirement and estate planning, college funding and long-term care. For exceptional cases, the firm maintains relationships with outside professionals specializing in such areas as real estate, wills and matrimonial law.

Business hours are from 8:30 — 6:00 Monday through Friday and from 11:00 — 3:00 on Saturday. For an appointment or to speak with an XYZ Financial Management representative, please call: 212.222.2222 or visit our website: www.xyzfinancial.com.

Note: Members of the press are invited for a private demonstration.

Chapter 3

Getting Read
The Power of Direct Mail

There's a reason you get so much mail—it works. It sells products—from life insurance to vacations, direct mail can give you a huge potential for profit. American Express does a ton of it. So does Fidelity Investments, Nationwide and TIAA-CREF. And in sales, yes, size matters, in fact, it matters very much. But creativity also matters when it comes to getting those envelopes opened and selling product.

Direct marketing, as opposed to "blind" generally non-creative "junk mail," (often addressed to "Resident") can help you sell more. With a targeted list and the right message you can use direct mail to promote a special event such as a retirement-planning seminar or to announce new hours, a new location, new personnel or virtually anything to draw attention to your business from the right prospects.

Having a seminar? Let the right customers know with a direct pitch. Having an expert speak on the virtues of retirement planning? A professional direct mailer can help you truly exploit this potential, generally at a low cost and probably with some innovative ideas you never would have considered on your own.

The Power of Numbers

In 2001, U.S. direct and interactive marketers generated an estimated $1.86 trillion in sales, an 8.9-percent increase over 2000. Catalog sales were up 8.2 percent, and Web-driven sales were up 7.9 percent. Ad spending also grew. In 2001, U.S. marketers spent an estimated $196.8 billion on direct-response advertising, a 3.6-percent increase over 2000. That growth is only about half the annual growth experienced over the past five years according to the Direct Marketing Association (DMA, http://www.the-dma.org), the oldest and largest trade association for users and suppliers in the direct, database and interactive marketing fields.

Direct marketing is one-to-one marketing. Its aim is to isolate you with the prospect. Therefore, you need a very targeted message and the right list. Your goal is to try to bring them into your office. What you know about them and how you choose to contact them will be critical. The payoff can be rewarding. There are high failure rates to this method but to minimize them, remember the two above-mentioned points— message and list power. But when direct mail works you can really strike the mother lode so it can pay to go with a pro. A lot has happened in this industry recently, making it wise to consider a consultant who can help you get beyond the write 'em and mail 'em from the kitchen table stage.

Direct mail can be easily confused with junk mail. It's not the same. While you may have visions of yourself and a few employees and possibly some soon-to-be former friends standing around a table in a crude assembly line folding, licking, sealing and stamping a stack of envelopes on a Saturday afternoon, professional direct mail is very different.

One financial advisor in California has been using a local, mail house for about 15 of the 28 years she's been in business. Among other things, she likes the bulk mail permit customers of mailing houses can use—drastically reducing postal costs. She does about two mailings annually but intends to do more. Her list of 2,000 was built by asking clients to sign up for news of upcoming events. Periodically, she "cleans" the list—removes names with invalid addresses.

"When we mail for an event we generally get a better than 50% attendance," she says using both postcards and e-mail. Occasionally, she hires a freelance artist and graphic designer to create a mail piece. Other times she's used postcards supplied by a product manufacturer. Postcards are cheap and have "staying power." E-mail's cheaper but is easily forgotten.

"We did a mailing when we moved two years ago," she recalls. "We used a cute postcard of antique advertising art. It got people's attention. We're only one-half mile away from our former location and people are still walking in with that card."

At another old shop in Connecticut, in the shadows of the Yale University campus, relying on mailings is being revived.

"The office changed hands nearly four years ago after 56 years of the same owner," says the new manager. "We use invitation-style mailings to get customers to events." The staff does the mailings itself and uses a 500-name, homegrown list so they know there's a "built-in" interest in the material. Turnout for their events is "very good," according to the manager, who adds that they plan on making direct mail a regular part of their marketing.

Getting Started

You've got to reach someone with your message. You need a list of names. Not just any names. What they call in the industry—"qualified names"—basically people who want your product or service. You can build your own list by simply leaving a spiral notepad by the receptionist and asking visitors to leave their name and address. This will help you reach people who already know you and means they've given their permission to be contacted—save the notebook. You can possibly make better customers from your existing ones this way.

However, to reach new clientele you may need to buy a list from a broker. Generally, you pay for the one-time use of a fixed amount of names. Your material is sent to a mail house, which then coordinates it with the list from the broker and distributes it. Always add a few "decoy" addresses to be sure everyone's being honest. Also, add some sort of return vehicle, i.e. a mail-in slip for a catalog or special offer so you can capture some of the names yourself. These will undoubtedly be good prospects. Other prospects can be ranked according to age, income, gender, geographic location, profession or product preference. If a customer is interested in 529 plans, maybe long-term care is in his/her future.

Another tip: insert a "name-of-a-friend" feature. This will help build names by recommendation. While these names were not directly furnished by the prospect, they are a "warm" lead, meaning they probably are interested in your product and will at least open your letter.

Hit the phonebook or get in touch with an industry association. Give them a call. The DMA can help you find a direct-mail company or consultant in your area. As a member, they need to be of high ethical standards. Most have a wide range of experience and will probably offer a great amount of ideas for getting out a fresh and productive message.

Getting It Opened

We all know the scenario. You grab your mail for the day and the first thing you do is throw out all the stuff you don't want or don't recognize. How does the mailer get past this? By being creative.

"The object of direct mail/response is to obtain a greater 'share of mind' of the prospect," says Elliott Black, president of EMBA, Inc., of Northbrook, IL, (www.embainc.com), a marketing-consulting and integrated-marketing communications firm serving business-to-business and business-to-consumer companies. "We've regularly used direct-response tactics for small businesses over the past 20 years."

As with all marketing programs, using an outside service to coordinate the program is essential, notes Black. "We can establish demographics of the targeted customer, obtain the appropriate mailing list and select the right mailing house to minimize costs and assure proper execution."

Black recommends postal cards as "very effective." The idea is to build awareness and name/logo recognition. The cards can equally be used as individual calls to action, he says.

Technology and Tradition

Bob Blackman of AmazingMail.com utilizes a combination of traditional mail supported by the Internet and full color to attract attention.

The AmazingMail Internet service allows you to create real full-color postcards on the Web that are printed and mailed the next business day. This is great for small businesses because there are no minimums. "You create and mail exactly the number you need and can change the images and messages any time," says Blackman, whose firm has helped many small businesses to efficiently promote themselves. Cards are printed and into the mail the next business day and the Web is convenient. Paper quality must be considered. For a postcard try 110 lb. paper, hi-gloss lamination. If you go it alone, talk to a printer about this but that's more time and money. Plus you can personalize as mail merge features allow you to automatically personalize every card. This can truly help separate your mail from the rest of the pack. AmazingMail will also host your images, address book and more. Prices are generally very reasonable, ranging anywhere from $1.25 for 1 to as low as $0.84 if you buy 1,000.

"While the mailing list itself is most important," says Black, "creativity is essential to get through the clutter."

Setting Goals

In developing a Direct Mail program, you first have to establish your objectives.

"Is it to build awareness? Is it to build store traffic? Is it to drive people to their Web site? Is it to promote a particular program or product? This will determine the direction to take," Black says. The creative approach follows.

"As with most marketing communications, it is frequency that becomes the driving factor. Sending one piece is like whistling in the wind," Black says. A campaign of at least three will bear the most fruit. "One particular technique that we have employed utilized postcards where each one was a part of a larger, suitable-for-framing poster. If the recipient brings all of the postcards to the office, they receive a copy of the poster."

Most direct mail marketing experts agree that a list broker can be your best friend.

The broker knows where to find lists and has inside information about sources, compilation and update procedures and should ask the right questions to the list owner to make sure the list is appropriate for the mailing. This can save time and avoid costly mistakes.

A mail house can save you time fighting with labels and lists and money on postage, plus provide the ability to select by interest or demographics. The marketer is then able to get his or her message directly into the targeted individual's mailbox and subsequently into their hand.

Keep in mind: Direct mail is the most measurable form of marketing. You can test a list and/or a mail piece and track the results. Once you know what works you can repeat it over and over again.

A Word on Privacy

Privacy remains a top issue in direct mail and continues to threaten the database-driven direct and interactive marketing industry. On Capitol Hill, there have been numerous movements to pass various types of privacy bills, including a "blended" type, meaning that consent would be required for health, financial and other "sensitive" data. Speak with a direct-mail consultant about privacy concerns before going ahead with any mailing.

Chapter 4

Getting Heard

Radio gives birth to a million images in a million brains.

Peggy Noonan, author

Work the Radio
Because the Ear Can Be Mightier than the Eye

Want to grow your sales? Better promote your business? Then turn on the radio.

Radio has helped thousands of companies and organizations of all sizes successfully increase sales and improve name recognition. Radio can serve as a stand-alone marketing effort or it can be a part of a larger, more comprehensive multi-media advertising plan encompassing print, television, direct mail and nearly every other form of promotion.

Consider that consumers spend about 85 percent of their time with "ear-oriented" media, such as radio, but spend only about 15 percent with "eye-oriented" media such as newspapers and magazines, according to the Radio Advertising Bureau (RAB), an industry association. This is a market ripe with potential.

Get to Know SAM

Who's SAM? SAM is the foundation of every complete radio marketing plan. SAM offers:

- Selectivity—target your best prospects
- Affordability—rates are often very reasonable
- Mobility—reach people wherever they are.

With radio advertising you can reach a substantial number of listeners on a daily, weekly or hourly basis. Radio listeners are often loyal and generally identify with just one or two stations or one or two programs. Correct station or program placement is crucial because when combined with the right advertising message, can drive customers to you.

Getting Started on Radio

The two basic questions to consider when thinking about getting your message on the airwaves are:

1. **What are you trying to sell?**
2. **To whom are you trying to sell it?**

When deciding what to discuss it's usually best to stick with one product or service on the radio. You can choose an area you're well established in or try one that you'd like to further develop.

You'll most likely be dealing in 30- or 60-second spots, so there's not a lot of time to discuss all the products and services your firm may offer. Therefore, it's generally a good idea to keep your talk limited to one simple and direct message.

If you want to promote investing for college, don't mention that you also offer long-term care insurance. If you want to attract people to a seminar, don't make an offer for a free newsletter at the same time—this can confuse the listener and doom your message. Once the prospect has shown interest you can offer other products and services.

Who are you trying to reach? This is as important as what you're trying to sell. To answer this question you'll need to know what the top radio stations are in your area and what are the most highly rated programs. Printouts illustrating Gross Rating Points (GRPs) and Cost Per Thousand (CPM) are worthless if you're airing the wrong program on the wrong stations.

Check a copy of the Broadcast Yearbook or the Standard Rate and Data Services Directory (SARDS). Both provide in-depth information about U.S. radio stations and are stocked at most public libraries. You can also call or visit potential radio stations and ask to see their copy. If you're a prospective advertiser, they should cooperate. You can also buy them at about $100 per copy.

Wisely Choose Your Audience

The next step is to choose the audience you want to reach. If you've never done radio before, it's generally recommended to begin in your own geographic region—test the local waters before branching out.

If you're trying to reach parents concerned about paying college tuition bills you'll need a program that reaches that audience. Rush-hour programming—morning and afternoon "drive times," generally from 6 a.m. to 9 a.m. and 4 p.m. to 7 p.m. are the most sought-after slots—and the most expensive—but are they the right times for you?

When someone is trying to get ready for work and get the kids off to school it may not be the best time to pitch a relatively complicated product in a short time period.

Most radio stations feature a business-news program. This is an obvious choice to promote most financial products but other programs may be just as effective and may offer better rates. Consider weekend and late-night/early-morning rates and all programs. Travel programs often offer very desirable demographics. Sports and business shows tend to attract male listeners. Contemporary music and entertainment programs usually reach younger people while news programs largely have an older audience. Traffic reports are important to commuters. Almost everyone pays attention to the weather forecast.

A station representative should be able to recommend the best programs for reaching your target audience. Ask to see the demographics on each program. These will tell you basic information such as listeners' age, gender and income. Often other information such as spending habits and outside interests are provided. You may find another program on a different time slot offering similar demographics at better rates.

What Do I Say?

When used as a form of communication to sell securities, radio advertising is regulated by the National Association of Securities Dealers (NASD). Check with your compliance department before submitting anything for broadcast.

If you want a unique message it may pay to hire a marketing firm. Radio messages are brief and to-the-point. They require skillful writing and industry or product knowledge. Ask the radio station for recommendations. A full-service agency will provide a copywriter, an account executive to manage your broadcasts, someone to produce your tape and advise you on such issues as whether to use an actor, your own voice or a station announcer.

A professional actor can give your message a mark of distinction that readers will recall and probably enjoy hearing. While your own voice can convey honesty you may sound amateurish. Using the station announcer often provides a seamless transition from the program to your message. Most radio stations, including those in big markets, provide professional scriptwriting, production and voice-over talent free of charge but you'll be committed to staying with that station.

Whichever you choose, maintain a serious tone. Managing money is serious business, a frivolous or comical tone is inappropriate and counter-productive.

Some Basic Questions:
- Will the radio station help write and produce your material?
- Have you gotten compliance approval?
- Is there a bonus advertising program, such as appearing on the station's website at a free or reduced rate?
- Are there reduced rates for greater frequency?
- Is there a "no-bump" policy?
- Will competitors air during the same program?
- If the station features a call-in financial show can you appear as a quest?
- Are the listening-audience figures independently audited?
- Have you included a point-of-contact i.e. telephone number, web address?

Sample Script

The following material will give you an idea of what a 30-second radio script is like. This script has not been approved for broadcast and appears strictly for educational purposes.

Sample Radio Script

[Radio ad: XYZ Financial Services]   [Running time: 30 sec.]

[Subject: Investing for Retirement]

[copy:] Are you concerned about meeting the high cost of retirement?

Will Social Security and personal savings be enough to help you live the kind of retirement lifestyle you've dreamed about and worked for?

Help's available at XYZ Financial Services.

An XYZ Financial Services representative will confidentially discuss the best ways to meet your long-term needs. We've been helping people like you with their financial futures for 15 years.

Stop by our office on 1234 Main St. in Townsville. We're open Monday through Friday from 9 a.m. 'til 6 p.m. and on Saturdays from 10 'til 3. There's no cost or obligation for the initial consultation.

You can also telephone us at 1-800-123-1234 or visit our website anytime at: www.XYZfinancial.com

Remember, it's your retirement. Let XYZ Financial help you enjoy it. [end sample script]

Analysis: The script above is simple and effective because it:
- Presents one problem—being able to afford retirement
- Offers one solution: a consultation with XYZ Financial—the sponsor
- Uses the words "you" and "your" seven times. Key words in person-to-person conversation
- Emphasizes experience and confidentiality
- Stresses there's "no obligation"
- Offers an incentive—a free consultation
- Gives several points of contact and hours of operation
- Provides name recognition and message recall—XYZ Financial is mentioned four times, including in the closing line.

Chapter 5

Getting Caught: A Few Words on Risk and Spin
Don't Want to 'Risk' It Then Don't 'Spin' It

Media relations can be fraught with "risk." They don't have to be but they often are. Generally, media relations are enjoyable and frequently help build a business' reputation but there are serious responsibilities associated with this and pitfalls to avoid. This is a fact of the business and in my experience, one few professionals are willing to discuss with potential clients. We'll come back to risk in a minute.

As for "spin," this is a word nearly everyone seems to like using—those who are qualified to do so and unfortunately, those who are not. In terms of marketing and media relations, but more notably the latter, spin has come to mean "spinning the truth" or twisting a story so that it portrays the subject in a favorable (or as favorable as possible) light. This is nothing new. What's new is the way it has entered the common vocabulary and is often considered an acceptable way of doing business. I suspect we generally have Washington, home to numerous media relations and image-consulting professionals, to thank for this—politicians have been spinning the truth to protect and expand their interests probably longer than any other group.

I've been in many media-relations discussions where the question, "How will we spin it?" is asked over and over again. By "it" they mean the message they're trying to convey, protect or change to their advantage and the question is usually posed by non-media-relations professionals. This is very concerning as deliberate "spinning" often is a very risky strategy to pursue.

Here's why...

You're considering "spinning" a story. This means you're probably altering the truth to your own advantage. As we said earlier, this is a common practice but usually not an ethical one. You may enjoy a short-term success but most likely will fail in the long term. The truth will almost always be found out—don't let it be to your disadvantage.

Most reporters become apprehensive simply because of reasons such as this—very often individuals do not tell them the "whole story" or only tell their version of events. That's why they often double-check and triple-check their sources of information—to make sure they're telling their readers the truth. If they don't, they'll damage their own reputation.

And it's usually very easy for a reporter to get to the truth. A good reporter will very rarely take one person's version of a particular story. They often ask for references and supplementary sources. If you're found out to be less than truthful, you're credibility and trust levels will be crushed—and not just in the reporter's eyes. Do not exaggerate. Do not evade the question or deliberately provide a superfluous answer hoping to throw the reporter "off the trail." If you cannot directly answer a question, state you're not comfortable with it or "not at liberty" to discuss such matters and then ask to move on. Do not feel pressured to say what you think someone "wants to hear." And do not feel that you must answer every question.

Spinning cannot only hurt any marketing and/or media-relations strategy you're pursuing but also damage your community reputation. And once damaged, reputations are very difficult to restore—in any profession but especially in financial services. Furthermore, it tarnishes the credibility of your entire profession.

Beware the Spin Masters

Be wary of any media-relations professional overly emphasizing a "spinning" strategy. What should be emphasized in any media-relations or marketing plan is your strengths and qualifications. If for example, you are not a tax-planning expert, don't advertise yourself as one despite how tempting the opportunity may appear. Stay away from areas where you're not qualified to comment.

Imagine the following scenario:

Your office telephone rings and it's a reporter asking about recent changes in the tax code for an article he or she is preparing for that weekend's business section of your town's newspaper. You see the opportunity and comment despite not being totally confident in your tax knowledge. The reporter is on deadline and as a fellow professional— trusts you and your judgment and doesn't double-check your answers for accuracy. Your comments appear in that weekend's edition. Readers see it and begin calling their accountants in regard to your comment or tax professionals call the reporter or his/her editor pointing out your error. Both yourself and the reporter are now looking foolish.

And don't believe that if nothing happens in the first 24-48 hours you're free. Letters and e-mails may start coming in. The rule-of-thumb is if one person called or wrote in about an error, chances are at least 10 others noticed it too. Also, people tend to save newspaper clippings for some time and once something is in print, it can come back to haunt you at any time—weeks, months, even years later. Imagine what this can do to your professional reputation and how the reporter who trusted you feels.

You may be one of the most ethical and hardworking business persons in the world but your integrity will have been compromised because you were too eager to see your name in print. And as we said earlier, your reputation will be very hard to repair. Very likely the loss to your business will be immeasurable.

As we mentioned earlier, simply tell whoever is asking that it's not your strong area and to please keep you in mind for ones that are—then name some of them and if possible, refer the reporter to a credible source in which you have confidence. It's also a good idea to tell the reporter to use your name as a "way of introduction" when calling the recommended source. The referral may result in business for you in the future. Most likely, the courtesy and thoughtfulness will be appreciated by both the reporter and the source, and your reputation will remain where it belongs—in a position of high esteem.

If a reporter asks what your fees are, disclose them. If they're negotiable depending on the amount of assets—say so. If you're not comfortable state that fees are kept confidential. The simple truth is, your opinion will be valued and your business will prosper by telling the truth.

Controversial Topics

You may be called on from time to time to comment on a controversial aspect of your business. Simply because a topic is deemed controversial does not mean you should avoid it. In fact, it's quite the opposite. Should you have a fair and knowledgeable position on a controversial issue, you may do yourself and your profession a favor by articulating it to the media. If you're truly well versed in such a topic and feel strongly about it, you may even engage in a friendly debate with someone taking the opposing viewpoint. Whatever you do, make sure your position is clear and that whatever statements you make are fair, accurate and easily understood.

Say you're asked to comment on a potentially controversial topic: What is your view on particular changes in the tax law? Is it fair to a certain set of people? What problems does the new tax code present? These types of questions are mildly controversial and by studying the new tax code you can probably come up with thoughtful answers to them. Questions on other subjects can, however, be much more provocative as you can see below:

What's your reaction to a recent industry scandal? What if yourself, a member of your firm or a business partner is involved in a scandal?

How do you react to questions like these?

While each of these situations is unique and warrants a special response, after examining the facts, your media-relations professional should be able to guide you through them by employing some general principles. If you or your firm is implicated in a scandal or other embarrassing situation, the prescription for this is commonly referred to as "damage control." Having worked as a media-relations professional and journalist on Wall St., I'm more than familiar with approaches to dealing with scandal and other embarrassing situations. It's a similar argument to the one made above on spin.

Take the worse-case scenario first—your name is associated with a business scandal. Here's a few action steps:

- **Examine the Facts**

  Is the allegation true or false? In other words, are you guilty or innocent?

  If it is true, the first thing you can do is literally nothing and hope it fades away with minimal damage. The second is to fight the charges by claiming it was "some misinterpretation of the facts." The risk here is you have to weigh the odds to see if your position is believable in the "court of public opinion."

  The third method is to take responsibility, apologize, make whatever amends are needed—moral, financial (i.e. pay fines) etc. and move forward.

  I generally advise the third approach: take responsibility, provide the reasons for your behavior, offer to make restitution and try to put the incident behind you as soon as possible. If the action concerns an employee or business partner, it may be necessary to terminate your relationship with him/her in order to salvage your own reputation.

  The silence that is inherent in doing nothing generally implies that you are indeed guilty and are just keeping a low profile in the hope that the entire affair will "blow over." A counter attack will probably do more harm than good in this case because as mentioned earlier, it's hard to argue with the truth and you'll probably only give "extended life" to a harmful story and further damage your reputation.

Similarly, saying you were "misquoted" is weak and almost never believed by your peers or the public. Plus, the reporter probably has the conversation taped or has notes from which he or she will refer should you argue for a correction. If you truly were misquoted or deliberately portrayed in a negative fashion you have a right to a retraction but this is rarely the case.

What follows are a few methods of self-defense in media-relations:

- **Take Direct Action**—Directly write, e-mail and/or telephone clients explaining your side of the story or hold a press conference or issue a press release to tell your side of it. Be clear and concise in this method. Do not get sentimental or emotional—state the facts and be prepared to support them with evidence. You can also put a similar and more comprehensive message on your web site, referring anyone interested in learning more to it should you decide to withhold comment.

  You can also call an editor or reporter directly and ask to tell your side of the story, as long as you have a legitimate story to tell.

- **Control the Message**—Make sure only one or two people from your office are permitted to speak with the media on all matters (see sample Press Relations Policy at the end of this chapter). During a media-relations crisis, this should be restricted to only one person—usually your media-relations professional. The reason for this is obvious: having several people authorized to publicly talk about a particular event to the public/news media is a prescription for disaster. You'll have little or no control over what information is being disseminated and probably be in a near-helpless position.

  For those who are permitted to speak, keep the message brief and to the point. Do not stray from topic even if asked by journalists to do so. Again, have evidence to support any claims. Do not be afraid to say something like, "I'm sorry, I cannot comment on that matter at this point as we're waiting for all of the facts to come in." A response like this shows you're being responsible and not "dodging the issue." Offer to get back in touch once you have your necessary information.

While there are risks associated with any media-relations policy, usually they will be minimal providing you adhere to a sound practice based on honest and direct communication and remain honorable in your professional conduct.

Sample Media Relations Policy

It is important that as a company, for reasons explained below, that we follow a simple media-relations policy. While the policy is clear, failure to adhere to it can have severely negative repercussions for individuals, for our firm and even for our industry and can possibly result in dismissal.

As a representative of our company, you may receive media requests for interviews, basic information about us (off- or on-the-record), a partner or client, quotes, fact verification, permission to attend/cover a company event or meet with personnel etc.

It is vital that any and all information transmitted to the media by any means; in person, over the telephone, fax or e-mail, be conveyed in a manner that is consistent with our corporate goals and policies. Any and all media requests are to be immediately forwarded to the Corporate Communications Dept. and your direct supervisor. Do not provide a response yourself. Under no circumstances is any information to be provided until the request is considered by management and the appropriate response is decided. There are no exceptions to this policy.

How to Respond to Media Inquiries

Should you receive a press inquiry, first ask for the caller's name, affiliation and telephone number. Inform him/her that you are not authorized to speak with media representatives but will pass his/her request to the appropriate individual. Then directly forward the request to our Corporate Communications representative or your direct supervisor. They will decide how to best handle the inquiry, often by directing the reporter to a subject-area expert.

Do not provide an "off-the-record" response. While it is understood that such a response shields the identity of the source, very often this does not provide adequate protection and the source is eventually discovered.

Those who do speak to the media without prior approval will be subject to disciplinary action. Any questions regarding this policy should be sent to our Corporate Communications representative.

Issuing Media Statements

No individuals, groups or departments are to issue media statements/press releases without proper review and approval from the Corporate Communications Dept. prior to release. Anyone interested in preparing a media statement or release should be prepared to submit a valid reason for doing so and allow at least 24 hours for internal review.

Summary

Media relations are an important part of our marketing and communications strategy and it is our intention to have a pleasant relationship with all members of the press.

How we are perceived in the media can influence our business. Obviously, positive media relations will help us maintain our reputation and attract quality individuals, both of which will grow our company. Inaccurate information can be harmful and may result in the wrong image being conveyed—potentially damaging our business and/or reputation.

We realize members of the media are working hard to provide a valuable public service which we appreciate and respect. It is our aim to have a fruitful relationship with them. Please keep this in mind.

Chapter 6

Getting Quoted: Talking to Reporters

O.k. Your media-relations plan is starting to bear fruit. The press release you distributed has generated calls from a couple of reporters who want to speak with you about your business. Now what?

Now you take the game to the next level.

If this is the first time you're being contacted, it's important to come to the phone as quickly as you can. Remember, the reporter still does not know you and he or she may call on another contact should you not be available. Nor should you pass the call on to someone else on your staff. If the reporter has asked to speak with you then you should come to the phone. If once the conversation gets underway you discover someone else in your firm is better suited to answer the questions, then it may be the right time to try to get that person to speak with the reporter then and there. Remember, time is often of the essence to reporters. If it's not possible, make a time to return the call and be sure you do so when you say you will.

When you are on the phone with a reporter, respect their time. Stick to the subject and don't use the conversation as an opportunity to start promoting other aspects of your business or to talk about your personal life.

When am I "Off" or "On the Record?"

Once a person identifies himself as a "reporter," you must operate with the idea that anything you say may appear in print. You're "on the record," unless otherwise stated. This includes not only your name and affiliation but any comments you make, even the spontaneous joke or casual observation.

"Off the record," means nothing you're about to say can be used in the story. You may provide this information for the reporter's background knowledge or to shield your name. Do not use "off the record" remarks to malign or disparage a competitor or organization with which you disagree or dislike. If the reporter insists he or she must have "on the record" material then it's probably best to politely end the conversation. You do not need to state why. You can simply say, "I'm not comfortable or authorized to comment on that. I hope we can work together again in the future on a different subject."

Be aware that material obtained "off the record" often shows up in the story. Don't be surprised by this. The reporter was probably able to verify the information from another source.

"Not for attribution," is different. A less used and slightly more confusing phrase, "not for attribution" indicates that you're not to be quoted but the reporter can use the information you've provided without identifying its source.

With both "off the record" and "not for attribution" it is up to you to make these demands. Having a person to quote adds responsibility and integrity to the story. While reporters generally dislike using anonymous sources, most will respect your wish. Their intentions are generally honorable—they regularly want to provide their readers with useful information. They do not want to embarrass you.

Also realize that if you make yourself available to the press by implementing a media-relations strategy, you're stating that you are prepared to speak with a reporter. While you have every right to expect reporters to stick to the subject area, occasionally stories stray off the topic. In those cases you must be prepared to professionally answer their questions and try to steer the conversation back to its original course. If it gets too far off the agreed-upon subject say something like: "I thought this interview was about tax planning. I'm not prepared to speak about the changes in the law you're bringing up."

Don't Ignore the 'Small Media'

There's big media and there's small media. "Big media" are the well-known newspapers and web sites, national magazines and radio, cable and network television stations. The "small media" are newsletters, local and regional radio stations and newspapers, limited circulation publications and special-interest websites.

But the small media is not small at all. Here's why. None of us start in the major leagues. Most so-called "big-time" reporters get their start in smaller, lesser-known media outlets, like their local newspaper or an obscure website. As they progress in their careers to better known media organizations it's not unusual for them to call on a source who helped them earlier—especially if that source was courteous and knowledgeable. Good sources make good reporters. So the young reporter who called you today from the website you never heard of may be calling you tomorrow from a regional business magazine and from a cable television station some time after that.

The second reason is that while the media outlet may in fact be a very small one, possibly a newsletter or website with a very narrow subscription base, it can very well be regularly read by other writers and editors seeking story ideas and sources to go with them. Editors are regularly looking for fresh story ideas—it's what sells newspapers. It's common for an editor to scan a story in a lesser-known publication and then give a similar assignment to a reporter in his or her organization. And they may very well call the same source for information—meaning potentially greater exposure for you and your business. This is why I recommend keeping a list of journalists you've worked with and periodically contacting them with a press release, e-mail or even holiday greeting card—to keep your name (and telephone number) "in front of them."

The third reason against ignoring lesser-known media is that other professionals are probably reading it. Say a reporter from a lightly circulated newsletter for accountants calls you on a story about tax professionals offering investment services. You give a thoughtful response based on your experience with this issue. It's very possible that once the story appears in print, an accountant who read the story and was impressed by your knowledge will call and ask you for some additional information. You may continue speaking with this person and a mutually beneficial business relationship may develop. He may refer some leads to you or you may partner with him or her on a project(s) or offer your expertise on a consultancy basis. And with the reach of the World Wide Web, there's no telling how far your name may travel and who may read about you, which brings me to my next point: When a reporter asks to speak with you—be you.

Be Yourself

When speaking to a lay audience, try not to be overly complicated. When speaking to a trade publication, it is acceptable, often it's even encouraged for you to maintain a more technical or complicated position. In either case, be sure you know your facts and also be sure the reporter has at least a basic grasp of the issues as well. It's perfectly acceptable to ask the reporter how comfortable he or she is with the topic and feel free to thoroughly explain your viewpoint, just don't stray from the topic. Reporters mainly want to be sure the information is fair, accurate and timely. By being a subject-matter expert and being clear in your remarks, you're making sure that the facts will be correctly reported. Be yourself, don't try to impress the reporter by being someone you're not.

While most reporters who cover a particular area (beat reporters) generally have a fair degree of knowledge on the subject, do not assume they are experts on it. They generally have a broad range of industry knowledge but will probably not be as well versed as a subject-matter expert. You may be an expert on IRA transfers. The reporter probably has a good understanding of IRAs and a basic knowledge of transfers but will most likely not know all the details on this issue. That's probably why he's speaking with you—to learn the relevant details and report them to his readers. Don't hesitate to give those details.

While reporters are generally knowledgeable about the subject, do not treat them like industry associates. Keep "shop talk" or jargon to a minimum. Do not assume they know as much as you do on the topic. Avoid industry slang and explain any abbreviations or other "trade words" you may use. Do not become arrogant or slighted if asked to elaborate on a particular response, the reporter is only seeking clarification to avoid a mistake. Instead, remain courteous and use the question as an opportunity to further demonstrate your knowledge.

While it sounds obvious, never respond with: "That's a stupid question." It may be clear to you because you deal with these issues on a regular basis but it may not be so to the reporter or his or her readers, who may not have the same level of expertise as you. It's generally better to take a few seconds to organize your thoughts and provide the response he or she is seeking. Nor should you speak too quickly, this is another very good way to have your message mixed. It's acceptable to stop and ask if the reporter is "getting this all down" or would he or she like you to repeat or elaborate on certain points.

You Advertise—So What?

Never expect preferential editorial treatment because your organization advertises in the publication for which you're being interviewed. The editorial and advertising departments are regarded as "Church and State," meaning one is not to influence the other. By asking for editorial coverage because you advertise (or might advertise) is insulting to the editorial staff members who are trying to remain unbiased in their reporting.

Some organizations keep advertising and editorial staffs on different floors to help avoid conflicts. While overlap between advertising and editorial staffs does exist in lesser publications, it is frowned upon within the industry and in journalism schools. The public quickly notices media organizations that openly provide editorial support to advertisers and they almost immediately lose faith in them, believing (probably correctly) that such news is not as fair and unbiased as it could be but favors the advertisers.

Similarly, do not attempt to "buy" yourself positive coverage by doing things like taking a reporter to lunch. Nor should you send a gift after a favorable story runs. It is acceptable to phone a reporter after a story appears, compliment him or her on their professionalism and offer to have lunch some time as long as you are not expecting any special future treatment. Some organizations have policies prohibiting reporters from accepting lunches, business trips or other items paid for by sources. Respect their professionalism by asking this in advance and do not be offended should they decline your invitation for professional reasons.

Close any interview by making yourself available for future questions. Offer a press kit if they do not already have one. Make your telephone and e-mail available for follow-up but do not ask to review the story before it goes to press. There generally is not time for this and the reporter will probably consider such a request offensive.

Chapter 7

Getting in Print
Submitting Newspaper and Magazine Articles

Writing for publication, much like hosting a radio call-in show, can be a great way to raise awareness of your business. While there are some parallels, writing a newspaper or magazine article is very different from crafting a press release. In addition to a list of other factors, which we'll get to in this chapter, primarily you'll need to be an authority on your subject matter.

The press release is about you, your office, some aspect of your business or your take on a particular subject or issue. The goal behind a newspaper, magazine or website article is to inform readers about a particular issue. Just as having your name positively portrayed in an article, authoring a submission can also add integrity to your image and help grow your business. Like other forms of media relations, it is not an advertisement. While promoting your firm is still the reason you're spending the time and energy to submit an article, it is secondary to the idea of conveying knowledge and information. You must be sincere about this if you are serious about submitting articles for publication.

Be Honest with Yourself

As a wise man once said, "Above all, to thine own self be true."

The first thing to consider when thinking about becoming an author is: Do I seriously have the time to do this in the way it ought to be done? Like anything else worthwhile, writing a good article takes time. While having a weekly column seems impressive, meeting that schedule can be very demanding.

You need to select a subject matter. Research it so you can knowledgeably write on it and find a publication interested in publishing it. This is how professional writers spend a good part of their days — researching markets, finding information and then writing and editing before submitting to a publication. We will not discuss how to write here because there are plenty of good books and courses on that subject. While not everyone writes well enough to be published chances are if you're knowledgeable about a subject, you'll be able to write with a degree of intelligence about it.

Most financial professionals who regularly submit articles do so for the promotional value—often they do so without pay. Also, any time you spend writing will be less time you have for other things, such as holding meetings with clients. Decide early whether the research, writing, rewriting and dealing with an editor is worth your time.

You may want to hire a "ghost writer," a professional who will write for a fee and allow you to submit it under your name. The risks with this idea are that you must find a qualified writer, pay him or her and then be prepared to answer any questions your editor may have about the work. No reasonable editor will knowingly allow a ghost-written story to appear in print. The editor is capable of hiring a freelance writer as well but is giving you the opportunity because of your expertise. If you decide writing an article is worth the effort, here's how to proceed.

Select Your Subject Matter

As we've noted earlier, stick with what you know. If you're a tax-planning expert don't try submitting articles on long-term care insurance. Once you decide on your topic, narrow it down. Tax-planning, for example, is a very broad area. Consider what areas in which you've developed a specific expertise. Is it tax-planning for seniors? Married couples? Corporations? Small-business owners?

Once you've narrowed down your subject, try to decide on a timely area. It's always attractive to an editor to have the chance to deliver something before anyone else has or to publish commentary on something new. Think about writing articles that clarify a possibly ambiguous situation. Aim to solve problems by educating the readers. For a consumer audience, do not be too technical or complicated but do not be overly simplistic either. When writing for a trade audience, you can venture into a subject's idiosyncrasies. Talking in advance with an editor should clarify how you should approach your subject matter. And since you're not a professional writer or reporter, don't try to sound like one when speaking with an editor. State early on exactly what your profession is and how your article may benefit the readers. You'll get ideas by examining changes in the law or tax code or by reviewing unusual cases. A sample "query letter," where you explain your article's value to an editor, follows this chapter.

Whatever you do, make sure you intimately know your subject

matter. Have someone review your work before submitting it for both grammar and information quality. Very often at smaller publications, editors will not have the resources to "fact check" your work and will rely on you as the "expert." As earlier mentioned, embarrassing an editor with incorrect information can damage the reputation of yourself and the publication. Be a sober critic of yourself. Does your article stick to its subject and deliver what it promised? If you're explaining the value of second-to-die insurance do you provide it? This is the biggest test you'll face when writing.

Is your grammar acceptable? While you may be an expert on a particular subject, if you submit work that's grammatically poor you will severely hurt your chance to be published. If you have the opportunity to submit illustrations such as charts or graphs with your story do so or advise the editor where they can be obtained. Also, check if you need compliance approval from your home office before submitting material for publication.

In the eyes of your clients and prospects, writing for a trade audience implies that you are an expert in a particular area among your peers. To get promotional value from it you'd need to get it in the hands of clients and prospects by either mailing copies or distributing them at events, such as seminars or framing copies and hanging them in your reception area. Publishing articles in a consumer magazine or newspaper does not carry this impression but generally reaches a much larger audience. You'll usually get to state your name, title, firm's name and town in the "tag line," usually a brief statement at the end of your article. Sometimes you can include a brief description of your firm's principle line of business. Don't ask the editor if you get a tag line, simply add it to every story you submit. The editor will decide whether to use or discard it.

Sample tag line: *Sam Sample is vice president of XYZ Advisors, a tax-planning firm in Dodge City.*

Finding Your Market

Once you decide whether to try submitting to trade or consumer publications, the next step is to find the right one. If you're aiming for a consumer publication, start locally. In addition to newspapers, there are often regional business magazines and other publications that may cover your geographic area. Check your newsstands for appropriate possibilities. Buy the publications and study them before contacting editors to be sure if your story idea is suitable. As earlier advised, although they usually boast gigantic circulations, it's generally recommended to avoid "free" publications and concentrate on those with a paid readership.

Unless your brother-in-law owns a newspaper, there really aren't any "short cuts" to getting published. You've got to do your homework: know your subject matter, research your markets and write well. Your local library should have several reference guides to help you find appropriate publications. Reference guides you can check are: *Bacon's Publicity Checker, Writer's Market,* and *Magazine Marketplace (MMP)* but there are many others. A basic Internet search should turn up numerous possible outlets.

Once you select a publication, it's generally the query letter that will pique the editor's interest in your story idea. Like a business letter, keep the tone simple and direct. Being mildly friendly is acceptable. Avoid any bombastic or grandiose language, especially when it comes to noting your qualifications. Be sure to address the editor with the correct title, have all names correctly spelled and use single space. After a brief introduction, get into your idea and why it's pertinent to the readers. Add your qualifications and phone number should he or she want to discuss your idea. If you've got other published clips, include one or two copies.

Extra! Sample Query Letter

[Date]
Peter Pencil
Associate Editor
Journal-News
Dodge City, KS

Dear Mr. Pencil:

April 15, "tax time," is fast approaching. There have been several changes in the tax code that may affect your readers, such as the change in deductible limits for small-business owners.

I am a tax advisor at XYZ Advisors in downtown Dodge City with nearly 20 years of experience helping small-business owners manage their tax liability. I would like to submit an article for possible publication in the Journal-News about these basic changes in the tax code that will affect a large number of business owners this year.

As I regularly counsel people on tax issues, I would write about this in a plain, easy-to-understand style for the Journal-News readers.

I am also a member of our Chamber of Commerce and the Tax Professionals Institute of America. I would be pleased to answer any questions you may have about this article or about my qualifications. Feel free to call me at the number below to further discuss this idea.

Thank you for your time and consideration.

Sincerely,

Sam Sample
Principle Tax Advisor

Summary

There are many other ways to generate positive publicity for your firm than mentioned here. Seminars, television appearances and book writing can each provide excellent exposure and business-building forums. The media-savvy professional will utilize all or most of them throughout his or her career.

Remember that the key word in media relations is "relations." When you choose to work with a media-relations professional or establish a working relationship with the news media, aim to develop as close a working partnership as reasonably possible. The more the two of you get to know each other the better and more fruitful your partnership will be. Keep in mind that for best results, you and your media-relations professional are to work like a team and that means regular practice, trust, steady communication and a liberal exchange of ideas. Be generous when offering your expertise and don't expect a quick return on your investment.

And like yourself, be sure to work with a highly ethical media professional. You need to be honest with your media-relations professional in your qualifications, as well as in your expectations and he or she owes you the same courtesy. Anything less can very easily become counter-productive. There are very few guarantees in this business, and a fair amount of risk associated with it. Therefore, be wary of anyone promising quick results. A good media-relations professional will collaborate with you and consider the risks and any other potential negatives before going forward with a plan. Like investing (and marriage), for best results, plan for a long-term commitment.

The most important things you can do to benefit from media relations is work hard, be consistent, informative and honest. Be available for reporters and editors who call. Respect their deadlines and other obstacles they may face in their jobs and in time, you'll see that they will generally do the same for you.

A lively media-relations program will reward you in many ways. You'll be gratified to see your name positively portrayed in print and when others who've seen it stop you on the street to compliment you or ask a question. After some time, you'll probably see an increase in business that can be attributed to your media-relations program. And most of all, you can take comfort in the fact that somewhere your thoughts and words are doing what they're meant to do—help someone better prepare for their financial future.

In the end, this is what makes all the difference.

About the Author

J oseph Finora a former financial journalist and editor, is a marketing and media relations professional. Based in New York, he's helped several blue-chip, as well as boutique financial-services firms and industry professionals develop productive media-relations programs. He views disclosing media-relations clients as a conflict of interest and keeps his list confidential.

In addition to basic media-relations counseling and placement services, he offers:

- Executive speechwriting
- Media coaching
- Press conferences
- Marketing consultation.

For further information, additional copies or a no-obligation consultation, visit: www.josephfinora.com or directly contact Joseph Finora at: jfinora@optonline.net.

All calls, consultations and client lists are kept confidential.